Communication Station

Learning Center Projects

Written by **Susan Babler**
Illustrated by **Gary Mohrman**

Totline® Publications
A Division of Frank Schaffer Publications, Inc.
Torrance, California

Managing Editor: Kathleen Cubley
Editor: Gayle Bittinger
Contributing Editors: Carol Gnojewski, Susan Hodges,
  Elizabeth McKinnon, Jean Warren
Copyeditor: Kris Fulsaas
Proofreader: Miriam Bulmer
Editorial Assistant: Durby Peterson
Graphic Artist/Layout Artist: Sarah Ness/Gordon Frazier
Cover Design: Brenda Mann Harrison
Production Manager: Melody Olney

ISBN: 1-57029-159-4
Library of Congress Catalog Number 97-62224
Printed in the United States of America
Published by Totline® Publications
Editorial Office: P.O. Box 2250
            Everett, WA 98203
Business Office: 23740 Hawthorne Blvd.
            Torrance, CA 90505

20 19 18 17 16 15 14 13 12 11 10 9 8 7 6 5 4 3 2 1

Introduction

Working at stations is a great way to introduce your children to new concepts, reinforce concepts already learned, practice skills, and have fun while learning. Station work also gives them opportunities to remember and follow directions and complete projects—important skills for future learning.

The station projects in this book, *Communication Station*, are centered around the theme of communicating, with chapters on visual, verbal, nonverbal, and written communication. There are also chapters with station projects for a post office communication center and a restaurant center. The final chapter has directions and patterns for a yearlong book project that each child makes about his or her year in kindergarten.

Each station project includes an objective for the lesson, a list of materials needed, directions for setting up the station, introductory information (if required), step-by-step instructions for making the project, and a teacher-directed follow-up. There are also reproducible worksheets and patterns to make each station quick and easy to prepare.

Most of the projects have been written as if one child were working in a station at a time. If you are planning to have more than one child working, simply adjust the materials as needed. Some projects require working with a partner. You may want to preselect partners for the children, or you may prefer to let them choose their own partners.

Because of the easy-to-set-up stations and unique reproducible pages, *Communication Station* will provide you and your children with many opportunities for communicating all year long.

Contents

Visual Communication

Mural of Hearts

Objective

Communicate through a group mural.

Materials Needed

❑ worksheet
❑ butcher paper
❑ scissors
❑ crayons
❑ pencil
❑ tape

Setting Up the Station

• Make a copy of the worksheet on page 9 for each child.
• Cut a long piece of butcher paper and hang it on a wall at your children's eye level.
• Set out crayons, scissors, a pencil, tape, and copies of the worksheet.

The Project

Explain the following steps to your children.

1. Select a copy of the worksheet.

2. Use the crayons to decorate each heart on the worksheet with a picture of someone you love.

3. Cut out the hearts and write your name on the back of each one.

4. Tear off two small strips of tape and tape your hearts to the butcher paper.

Follow-Up

Write "We Love With Our Hearts" on the butcher paper. Talk about how everyone can tell who the children love just by looking at the mural.

Story Scroll

Objective

Tell a story on a scroll.

Materials Needed

❏ worksheet
❏ paper towel tubes
❏ butcher paper
❏ scissors
❏ glue
❏ tape

Setting Up the Station

- Make a copy of the worksheet on page 11 for each child.
- Collect two paper towel tubes for each child. You may wish to ask each child to bring two or more in from home.
- Cut butcher paper into 6-by-18-inch strips.
- Set out the paper towel tubes, butcher paper strips, scissors, glue, tape, and copies of the worksheet.

Introducing the Project

Show your children pictures of scrolls that were used in the past. Let them unroll and roll up a scroll you have made. Talk about how a scroll is similar to and different from a book.

The Project

Explain the following steps to your children.

1. Select a copy of the worksheet and cut out the story squares.
2. Arrange the squares in order and glue them on one of the paper strips. Allow the glue to dry.
3. Tape a paper towel tube to each end of the paper strip.
4. Roll the paper strip around the tubes to make a scroll.

Follow-Up

Let the children "read" their stories to you. Let them take their story scrolls home to read to family members. Encourage the children to draw their own stories to put on scrolls.

A Stitch in Time

Objective

Communicate ideas on fabric.

Materials Needed

❑ worksheet
❑ fabric
❑ scissors
❑ pencil
❑ fabric crayons
❑ apron
❑ fabric items

Setting Up the Station

• Make a copy of the worksheet on page 13 for each child
• Cut solid-colored fabric into 7-inch squares.
• Set out the fabric squares, a pencil, fabric crayons, apron, and copies of the worksheet.

Introducing the Project

Show your children a variety of items made out of fabric (a quilt with a diamond pattern on it, a T-shirt with a printed message on it, a fancy pillow with fringe, etc.). Ask them to tell you something about each item: "The quilt has a diamond. The T-shirt says, 'Have a nice day.' The pillow looks too fancy to sleep on." Tell the children that they will each have a fabric square to decorate. The squares will be put together to make a wall hanging for the room.

The Project

Explain the following steps to your children.

1. Put on an apron.

2. Select a copy of the worksheet.

3. In the square on the worksheet, write your name, then sketch what you want to draw on your fabric square.

4. Select a fabric square.

5. Write your name on it with one of the fabric crayons.

6. Carefully draw your picture on the fabric square using the fabric crayons.

7. Place your fabric square in the designated place. Recycle or take home your worksheet.

Follow-Up

Follow the directions on the fabric crayon box for setting the crayon onto the fabric (if needed). Put the squares together to make a wall hanging. (They can be sewn together, glued together, or even taped together.) Invite your children to admire their work and think about the many messages their wall hanging is communicating.

Write your name in the square.
Draw the picture or design you
want to put on your fabric square.

Stamp a Story

Objective

Tell a story with rubber stamp designs.

Materials Needed

- ❑ worksheet
- ❑ rubber stamps
- ❑ ink pads
- ❑ scissors
- ❑ stapler
- ❑ pencil

Setting Up the Station

- Make a copy of the worksheet on page 15 for each child, plus one for yourself.
- Collect three or four rubber stamps of animals and other characters.
- Using your copy of the worksheet, make a Stamp a Story book.
- Set out the rubber stamps, ink pads, scissors, stapler, a pencil, and copies of the worksheet.

Introducing the Project

Show your Stamp a Story book to your children. Talk about how the rubber stamp pictures on the pages tell the story. What did your rubber stamp character do first? Second? Third? Last?

The Project

Explain the following steps to your children.

1. Select a copy of the worksheet and cut out the pages.

2. Arrange the pages in order on the table.

3. Select one of the rubber stamp characters. Decide what it will be doing on the first page, and stamp it in that position. Continue with the other pages.

4. Collect the pages in order and staple them together.

5. Write your name on the back of your book.

Follow-Up

Let the children share their stories in small groups. Did anyone stamp the same story? Have them take their stories home to read to their families.

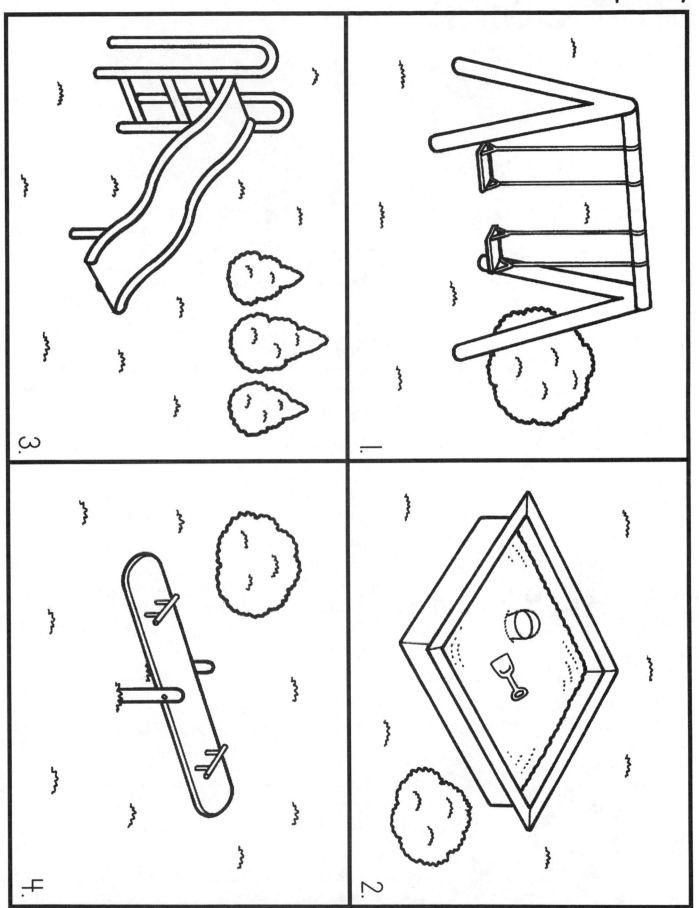

Sign Game

Objective

Recognize and learn the names of common signs.

Materials Needed

❑ worksheets
❑ crayons
❑ clear self-stick paper
❑ scissors

Setting Up the Station

• Make four copies of each of the worksheets on pages 17 and 18.
• Make one copy of the worksheet on page 19. In the two blank boxes on the copy, draw in two familiar signs common in your area. These could be important signs at your school, signs from favorite restaurants, or other traffic signs you would like to have included in the game. Make four copies of this worksheet.
• Cover all 12 pages with clear self-stick paper (or have them laminated).
• Cut out the individual boxes to make cards, and place them in the station.

Introducing the Project

Show the cards to your children. Help them name the sign on each card. Let them think of other signs they see around the classroom, school, and town. Discuss how to play the game Go Fish. Let the children tell you the rules of the game.

The Project

Explain the following steps to your children.

1. Working with a partner, turn all of the cards upside down on the table.
2. Play Go Fish.
3. The person with the most matches at the end of the game wins. Play another game, if time allows.

Follow-Up

Let the children decorate signs to hang up in the room. Give them large, precut shapes of stop signs, yield signs, crosswalk signs, and so on. Talk about what each sign means.

Verbal Communication

What Did They Say?

Objective

Look at pictures of people in action and think about what they might be saying.

Materials Needed

❑ worksheet
❑ pictures of people interacting
❑ scissors

Setting Up the Station

• Make a copy of the worksheet on page 23 for each pair of children.
• Hang up pictures of people interacting.
• Set out scissors and copies of the worksheet.

Introducing the Project

Show your children the pictures of people interacting. Discuss how the people are communicating. What do the children think they are saying?

The Project

Explain the following steps to your children.

1. With a partner, select one of the copies of the worksheet and take turns cutting out the picture squares.

2. Mix up the picture squares.

3. Choose one of the picture squares, look at it carefully, and decide what the people in the picture are saying to one another.

4. Show the picture to your partner and tell him or her what you think the people in it are saying.

5. Let your partner select a picture square and tell you what he or she thinks the people in it are saying.

6. Take turns with the remaining picture squares.

7. Divide up the picture squares to take home.

Follow-Up

Select simple comic strips or books with lots of conversation to read to your children. Talk about the various things people say to one another.

News Time

Objective

Practice communicating ideas through a pretend television news report.

Materials Needed

❑ worksheet
❑ VCR
❑ television
❑ blank videotape
❑ pencils
❑ pretend microphone
❑ video camera (optional)

Setting Up the Station

- Make a copy of the worksheet on page 25 for each child.
- Set up a VCR and a television and load the videotape.
- Videotape a real, child-appropriate television news report.
- Prepare the videotape to play it for the children.
- Set out a pretend microphone. This could be a microphone you have made from a cardboard tube and aluminum foil, or it could be a nonworking microphone from an old tape recorder.
- Put out pencils and copies of the worksheet.

Introducing the Project

Show your children the video of the news report. Talk about what the newscaster said and did. How did he or she tell the story? What was the report about? Tell the children that they will be creating their own news reports about what happens in kindergarten. Ask them to brainstorm the various kinds of events they could report on: recess activities, what letter of the alphabet they are studying, what their latest art project is, where they went on their last field trip, and so on. It may help to do your own short report about a current happening in your classroom, so they understand what to do.

The Project

Explain the following steps to your children.

1. Working with a partner, think about what topics you would like to report on.

2. Pass out copies of the worksheet to both of you. Make notes or draw pictures on it to remind you of your story.

3. Take turns talking into the microphone and making your news reports.

Follow-Up

The children who wish to can make their news reports in front of the whole class. If possible, videotape the reports so everyone can watch them together.

WKDG News Report
Channel 6

Storytime

Objective

Practice listening skills.

Materials Needed

❑ worksheet

❑ scissors

❑ stapler

❑ tape recorder with headphones

❑ blank cassette tape

❑ bell (optional)

❑ pencil

Setting Up the Station

• Make a copy of the worksheets on pages 27, 28, and 29 for each child, plus one for yourself.

• From your copy of the worksheets, cut out the story pages. Staple them together to make a book for yourself.

• Tape-record a simple story of "The Three Bears," describing the action on each page. At the end of each page, pause and ring a bell or say "Please turn the page," allowing the children time to turn the page.

• Set up a tape recorder with headphones.

• Make sure the story tape works and that the volume is adjusted appropriately.

• Set out scissors, stapler, a pencil, and copies of the worksheets.

The Project

Explain the following steps to your children.

1. Select a copy of each of the worksheets and cut out the story pages. You should have 12 small pages.

2. Put the pages in order and staple them together.

3. Write your name on the back of your book.

4. Put on the headphones and push the "play" button on the tape recorder.

5. Listen to the story and follow along in your book.

6. Rewind the tape when it is finished.

Follow-Up

Divide the children into pairs. Let them take turns telling the story to each other. Or, tell the story as a class. Have the children take their stories home to "read" and tell to their families.

The Three Bears

I'll Call You

Objectives

Practice communicating over the telephone.

Materials Needed

❑ worksheet
❑ two telephones

Setting Up the Station

• Make a copy of the worksheet on page 31 for each child. These will be sent home.

• Collect two sturdy play phones or nonworking telephones (with any long cords cut off).

The Project

Explain the following steps to your children.

1. Working with a partner, sit by the phones at the station.

2. Dial your partner's "phone number" on one of the phones. (The phone number can be real or make-believe.) Make a ringing sound and wait until he or she answers the phone.

3. Talk to your partner on the telephone.

4. Hang up and let your partner call you.

Follow-Up

Help your children learn their phone numbers if they don't already know them. If area codes are needed to make local calls in your city, be sure to teach the children their area codes as well. Send the copies of the worksheet home with the children so they can make their own personal phone books.

Cut out the pages and staple them together.
Help your child fill in the name and phone
numbers of people he or she might call.

Name

Phone Number

Name

Phone Number

Name

Phone Number

Name

Phone Number

Nonverbal Communication

Face Talk

Objective

Explore how to communicate ideas through facial expressions.

Materials Needed

❑ worksheet
❑ clear self-stick paper
❑ scissors
❑ hand mirror

Setting Up the Station

- Make a copy of the worksheet on page 35 for each child, plus one for yourself. Save the children's copies to send home with them.
- Cover your copy of the worksheet with clear self-stick paper (or have it laminated). Cut out the boxes to make individual feeling cards.
- Set out the feelings cards and a hand mirror.

The Project

Explain the following steps to your children.

1. Working with a partner, sit down at the station.

2. Choose one of the feelings cards. Look at it without showing it to your partner. Decide what feeling the card is showing.

3. Hold the mirror in front of your face and make an expression that demonstrates the feeling shown on the card.

4. Let your partner see your expression and guess what feeling you are showing.

5. Show your partner the feelings card and make that kind of face together.

6. Take turns selecting cards and making faces until all of the cards have been used.

7. If there is time left, mix up the cards and play again.

Follow-Up

Talk about the way our faces can express our feelings. Read books about feelings. Send home a copy of the worksheet with each of the children so they can play this game with their families.

happy

sad

mad

excited

frustrated

worried

tired

surprised

scared

Sign Language

Objective

Learn about communicating with sign language and finger spelling.

Materials Needed

❑ worksheet
❑ sign language posters or books
❑ mirror (optional)
❑ scissors
❑ glue

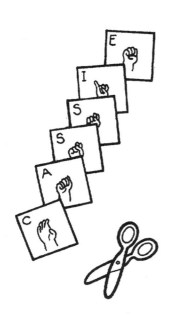

Setting Up the Station

• Make copies of the worksheet on page 37. You will need about two worksheets per child.
• Hang up sign language posters or set out books about sign language.
• Set up a freestanding mirror, if you have one.
• Set out scissors, glue, and copies of the worksheet.

Introducing the Project

Introduce your children to the idea of communicating with their hands. What are some ways they already do this? (Wave hello and goodbye, say how old they are, say stop, etc.) Following the pictures on the worksheet, teach them the signs for the phrase "My name is." Practice them together. Tell them that at the station they will learn how to sign the letters of their names.

The Project

Explain the following steps to your children. You may want to have an adult helper at this station.

1. Select a copy of the worksheet.

2. Cut off the sign language alphabet.

3. Look for the letters in your name and cut them out. If you need more than one of a letter, cut them out of extra worksheet copies.

4. Glue the letter signs on the line so they spell your name.

5. Practice finger spelling your name using the letter signs. Watch yourself in the mirror.

6. Use sign language and finger spelling to say the whole sentence "My name is _____."

Follow-Up

Have the children sign their names to each other. Together, use a sign language book to learn signs for familiar words. Let the children take their worksheets home.

My

name

is

✂ --

A	B	C	D	E	F
G	H	I	J	K	L
M	N	O	P	Q	R
S	T	U	V	W	X
Y	Z				

Animal Moves

Objective

Communicate a concept using only movements and gestures.

Materials Needed

❏ worksheet
❏ clear self-stick paper
❏ scissors

Setting Up the Station

- Make one copy of the worksheet on page 39, plus one copy for each child to take home.
- Cover one copy of the worksheet with clear self-stick paper (or have it laminated).
- Cut out the boxes to make the animal picture cards.
- Set out the animal picture cards.

Introducing the Project

Show your children ways to act out ideas without saying a word. Pretend to climb stairs or go to sleep. Can they guess what you are doing? Ask them to pretend to be an animal, such as a dog. What would they do? Let them practice acting out different ideas.

The Project

Explain the following steps to your children.

1. Working with one or two partners, put the animal cards in a pile face down in the middle of the table.
2. Select one of the cards and look at the animal picture on it without showing it to anyone else.
3. Begin to move about as though you are that animal. Remember to keep quiet. Ask the others to try to guess what animal you are.
4. If they cannot guess, try adding some other movements.
5. If they still can't guess, make the animal's sound.
6. When they guess correctly, the next person gets to take a turn.
7. Continue until all of the cards have been used.

Follow-Up

Send home copies of the worksheet with your children so they can play the game with their families.

Let's Do the Hula

Objective

Learn how ideas can be communicated through dancing.

Materials Needed

❑ worksheets
❑ mirror
❑ Hawaiian music
❑ Hawaiian maps, posters, or books
❑ grass skirts (optional)
❑ leis (optional)

Setting Up the Station

• Make one copy of each of the worksheets on pages 41, 42, and 43.

• Cut out the pictures of the hula dance movements from the worksheet copies. Hang these up in the station.

• Set up a full-length mirror.

• Select Hawaiian music (available at your local library). Prepare the music for playing.

• Arrange Hawaiian maps, posters, or books in the station. (Travel agencies are a good source for these.)

• If you wish, set out real grass skirts and leis (available at costume supply stores). Or, make your own grass skirts out of strips of green crepe paper and leis out of paper flower shapes threaded onto yarn.

Introducing the Project

Talk with your children about the hula dance. Explain that Hawaiian dancers use their bodies and hands to tell stories. Demonstrate some of the movements and have the children follow along.

The Project

Explain the following steps to your children.

1. Working with a partner, look at the Hawaiian materials at the station. Put on the grass skirts and leis, if available.

2. Together, try some of the dance movements shown on the worksheet pictures.

3. When you both feel like you are ready to tell a story with your hula dancing, turn on the Hawaiian music and begin.

Follow-Up

Let the children who wish join you in a group session of hula dancing. Watch a video of hula dancers telling a story. As a group, make up your own moves to tell your own story.

Hawaii

Love

Waterfall

Rain

Sun

Fish

Musical Art

Objective

Listen to music and communicate through drawing.

Materials Needed

- ❑ worksheet
- ❑ classical music
- ❑ tape recorder with headphones
- ❑ crayons
- ❑ pencil

Setting Up the Station

- Make a copy of the worksheet on page 45 for each child.
- Select a piece of classical music.
- Set up a tape recorder with headphones in the station.
- Put the tape of classical music in the tape recorder. Make sure everything works and that the tape is rewound. Adjust the volume appropriately.
- Set out the tape recorder, crayons, a pencil, and copies of the worksheet.

Introducing the Project

Play some classical music for your children. Ask them to listen carefully and think about what the music is "saying." Does the music sound happy, sad, or angry? Does it make them want to dance or march or go to sleep? Explain that there is no one right answer. The same music can make people feel differently. Let them move in place as they listen.

The Project

Explain the following steps to your children.

1. Select a copy of the worksheet and some crayons.
2. Write your name at the top of the worksheet.
3. Put on the headphones and turn on the tape.
4. Listen carefully while you draw to the music. Does the music make you want to draw long, flowing lines or short, choppy lines? What color does the music remind you of?
5. When the music is finished, rewind the tape.

Follow-Up

Talk with the children one at a time and let them dictate their response to the phrase at the bottom of their worksheet "When I listen to this music I feel _____."

Name_____

When I listen to this music I feel _____.

Puzzle Talk

Objective

Work with a partner and complete a puzzle without speaking.

Materials Needed

❑ worksheet
❑ rubber cement
❑ heavy paper
❑ clear self-stick paper
❑ scissors

Setting Up the Station

- Make one copy of the worksheet on page 47.
- Use rubber cement to stick the copy of the worksheet to a sheet of heavy paper. Cover the paper with clear self-stick paper (or have it laminated).
- Cut the prepared worksheet into an even number of interlocking pieces (4 to 8) to make a puzzle.
- Set out the puzzle pieces.

Introducing the Project

Talk with your children about cooperating and working with a partner. Have them think of ways they could communicate with someone without using their voice. Demonstrate this to them by asking them (without speaking) to do a simple exercise so many times. Let them take turns thinking of things to say without spoken words.

The Project

Explain the following steps to your children.

1. Working with a partner, sit down at the station and stop talking.

2. Using hand gestures and facial expressions to communicate, divide up the puzzle pieces and put the puzzle together.

3. When the puzzle is completed, congratulate each other—without words!

Follow-Up

Let the children think of ways to communicate basic classroom rules without using words. What could be a way to signal "Be quiet, please" or "Please sit down"?

Written Communication

Quills

Objective

Experiment with using a quill and paint to write.

Materials Needed

❑ worksheet
❑ feathers
❑ washable paint
❑ baby food jar
❑ plain paper

Setting Up the Station

• Make a copy of the worksheet on page 51 for each child.
• Collect large, clean feathers to use as quills.
• Pour a small amount of dark-colored washable paint into a baby food jar.
• Set out the feathers, jar of paint, plain paper, and copies of the worksheet.

Introducing the Project

Show your children a feather. Tell them that, long ago, people used feathers to write. Ask them to guess which part of the feather they used—the soft feathery part or the hard, pointy part. This kind of pen was called a *quill*. Demonstrate how to use a quill to write: dip the hard, pointy end in paint, then put it on the paper to make your mark.

The Project

Explain the following steps to your children.

1. Choose the quill you would like to use.

2. Select a piece of plain paper.

3. Dip the quill into the paint and make a few marks. Experiment writing with the quill on plain paper.

4. Select a copy of the worksheet.

5. Use the quill and paint to write your name at the top of the worksheet and complete the dot-to-dot picture.

6. Set your worksheet in the designated place to dry.

Follow-Up

Talk with the children about using the quill and paint. Was it easier or harder than using crayons or pencils? What did they like about using a quill? What did they not like about it? What other natural items could they use to write with? (Sticks, flower stems, pointed rocks, etc.) Let them take their quill pictures home.

Name_____

Connect the dots to complete the picture.

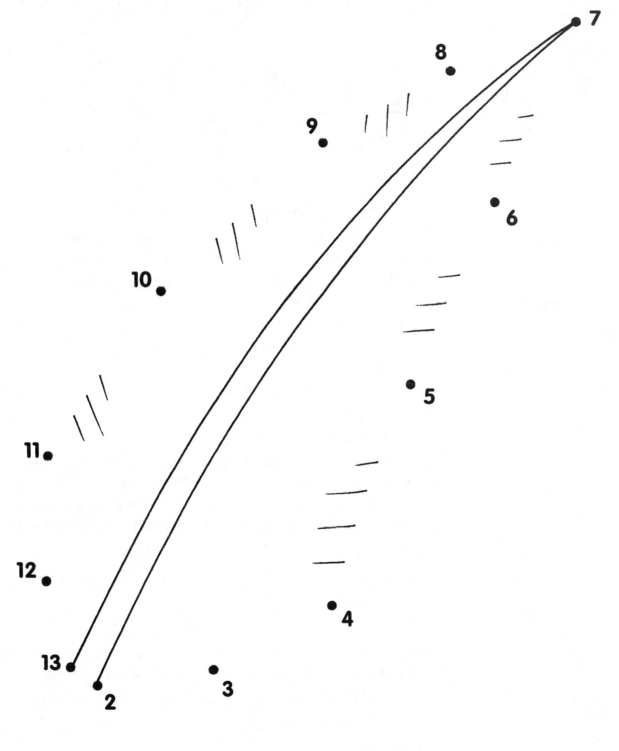

Fountain Pens

Objective

Experience using a fountain pen to write.

Materials Needed

- ❏ worksheet
- ❏ fountain pen
- ❏ ink
- ❏ ink well (if needed)
- ❏ plain paper
- ❏ apron

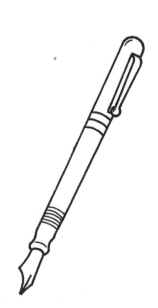

Setting Up the Station

- Make a copy of the worksheet on page 53 for each child.
- Purchase or find a fountain pen and the ink it needs, either an ink cartridge or ink and an ink well. (Fountain pens and accessories are available at office supply and art supply stores.)
- Make a demonstration poster by writing letters, numbers, and shapes on plain paper with the fountain pen.
- Hang up your examples.
- Set out the fountain pen and ink, plain paper, an apron, and copies of the worksheet.

Introducing the Station

Explain to your children how the fountain pen works. Show them how the ink flows out of the tip of the pen. Demonstrate how the ink runs and smears when it is wet. Explain that the ink will stain their clothes, and caution them to use great care when working with the fountain pen.

The Project

Explain the following steps to your children. You may want to have an adult helper at this station.

1. Put on the apron to protect your clothing.
2. Select a copy of the worksheet. Use the fountain pen to write your name at the top. Follow the outlines on the worksheet with the pen.
3. Set your worksheet in the designated place to let the ink dry.
4. On plain paper, continue experimenting with how the pen works.

Follow-Up

Ask the children questions about using the fountain pen: Would you like to do all your work with a fountain pen? Why or why not? What is fun about using a fountain pen? What is difficult? Let them take their fountain pen work home.

Name_____

Trace these lines using your fountain pen.

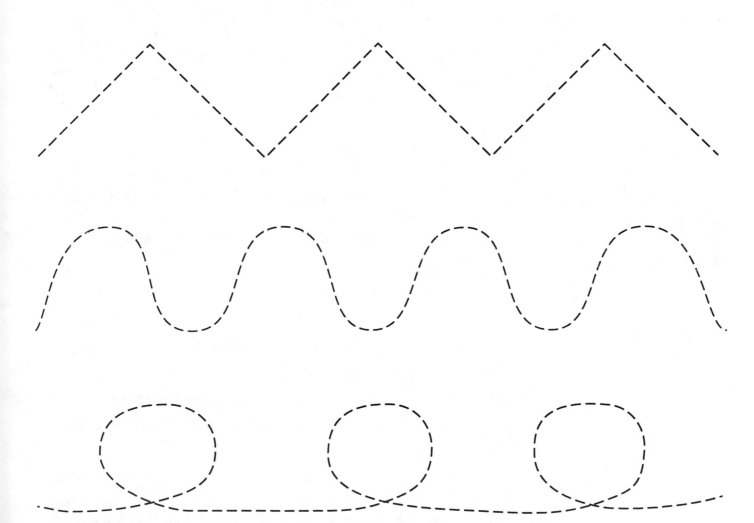

Writing With Pens

Aa Bb Cc

Objective

Experiment with writing using a variety of pens.

Materials Needed

❑ worksheet

❑ pens

❑ plain paper

Setting Up the Station

• Make a copy of the worksheet on page 55 for each child.

• Collect an assortment of pens, such as ballpoint, felt tip, thin line, thick line, and highlighter.

• Set out the pens, plain paper, and copies of the worksheet.

The Project

Explain the following steps to your children.

1. Select several pens you would like to try.

2. Use the pens to make marks, designs, or letters on the plain paper.

3. Select a copy of the worksheet.

4. Use one of the pens to write your name on the worksheet.

5. Choose a different pen to draw the required shape in each square.

Follow-Up

Help the children count how many different pens they had to choose from. Ask them what they liked and did not like about using these pens. Which one was the messiest? Which one drew the nicest lines? Let them take home their papers.

Name_____

Use a pen to draw the picture in each square.

Draw a [◯].	Draw a [▢].
Draw a [△].	Draw straight [——].
Draw a [∿].	Draw yourself [🙂].

Pencils

Objective

Use pencils to write a letter.

Materials Needed

❑ worksheet
❑ pencils
❑ letter sent to you

Setting Up the Station

• Make a copy of the worksheet on page 57 for each child.
• Collect a variety of pencils (regular, large, colored, mechanical, etc.).
• Make sure all of the pencils are sharpened.
• Set out the pencils and copies of the worksheet.

Introducing the Project

Ask your children if they have ever received a letter. How did they know the letter was for them? How did they know who had sent the letter to them? Talk about a few parts of letters: the greeting, the body or message, and the closing. Show them a letter that was sent to you. Point out these three parts of your letter.

The Project

Explain the following steps to your children.

1. Select a copy of the worksheet.
2. Think about who you would like to write a letter to.
3. Write the person's name at the top of the page.
4. Draw or write a message in the middle of the page, using as many different kinds of pencils as you can.
5. Sign your name at the bottom.

Follow-Up

Ask the children about the pencils they used. Which ones did they like the best to write with? How many pencils did they use to write their letters? Let them deliver their letters to the recipients, if possible.

Dear _____,

Love, _____

Keyboards

Objective

Become familiar with using a computer or typewriter keyboard.

Materials Needed

❑ worksheet

❑ clear self-stick paper

❑ scissors

❑ hole punch

❑ metal binder ring

❑ typewriter or computer and printer

❑ plain paper or computer paper

Setting Up the Station

- Make one copy of each of the worksheets on pages 59, 60, and 61.
- Cover the worksheets with clear self-stick paper (or have them laminated).
- Cut out the squares and punch a hole at the top left-hand corner of each square.
- Thread the squares onto a metal binder ring to make a simple dictionary.
- Set up a typewriter or computer and printer in the station, and put out the appropriate paper.
- Place the prepared dictionary in the station.

Introducing the Project

Show your children the keyboard on a typewriter or a computer. Point out all the letters and numbers on it. Ask them to find certain letters. Explain how to operate the typewriter or computer.

The Project

Explain the following steps to your children. You may want an adult helper to supervise this station.

1. Make sure the paper is ready for your work.

2. Practice keyboarding all sorts of letters and numbers.

3. Find the letters in your name and press them to write your name.

4. Look in the dictionary to find other words that you would like to print on your paper. Include other words you know.

5. Take your paper out of the typewriter or print it from the computer.

Follow-Up

Have the children look at all of the words they have written. Which ones can they read? Keep the dictionary to use for the Read a Book station on page 74.

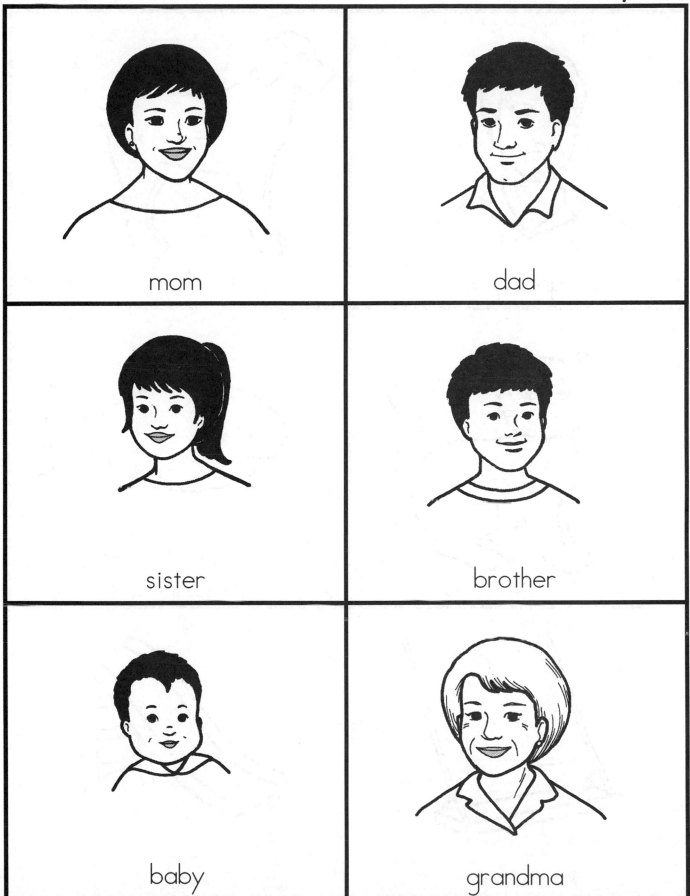

mom

dad

sister

brother

baby

grandma

grandpa

dog

cat

fish

swing

slide

bike

blocks

doll

hat

coat

boots

Letters

Objective

Write names with alphabet rubber stamps.

Materials Needed

❑ worksheet

❑ paper

❑ felt tip marker

❑ clear self-stick paper

❑ set of rubber stamp alphabet letters

❑ washable ink pad

Setting Up the Station

- Make a copy of the worksheet on page 63 for each child.
- On a sheet of paper, use a felt tip marker to write the first name of each child in your class.
- Cover the name sheet with clear self-stick paper (or have it laminated).
- Set out the name sheet, rubber stamp letters, ink pad, and copies of the worksheet.

The Project

Explain the following steps to your children.

1. Select a copy of the worksheet.

2. Using the rubber stamp letters, stamp your name at the top of the worksheet.

3. Look at the list of students on the name sheet.

4. Choose the name of a friend you would like to stamp on your list.

5. Look for the letters that spell the name, and stamp them on one of the lines on your worksheet.

6. Repeat with other friends' names.

Follow-Up

Let the children show you their lists and read the names to you.

Name_____

Map Symbols

Objective

Introduce the use of symbols to communicate.

Materials Needed

❑ worksheet
❑ map
❑ pencil

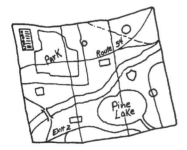

Setting Up the Station

- Make a copy of the worksheet on page 65 for each child.
- Find a map that uses symbols for places such as parks, schools, and fire stations.
- Set out a pencil and copies of the worksheet.

Introducing the Project

Show your children the map. Point out the symbols used on the map. Explain that symbols are sometimes used to communicate an idea or word, rather than writing out the actual words or word.

The Project

Explain the following steps to your children.

1. Select one of the copies of the worksheet and write your name on it.

2. Look at the map symbols on the worksheet. There are symbols for trees, houses, stores, parks, schools, and stoplights.

3. Look at the map of the town. Think about where you would like to have trees, houses, stores, parks, and schools.

4. Add the symbols to the map to create your own town.

Follow-Up

Display the children's maps. Let them look at each other's towns. Can they think of other places, and the symbols to go with them, to add to their towns?

Name_____

house ☐   store ◯   tree △

school ▭   park △   stoplight 🚦

Braille Alphabet

Objective

Learn about Braille, the writing system used by vision-impaired people.

Materials Needed

❑ worksheet
❑ cardboard
❑ paper clip
❑ book or other material written in Braille
❑ construction paper
❑ pencil
❑ glue in squeeze bottle

Setting Up the Station

- Make one copy of the worksheet on page 67.
- Turn the worksheet over and place it on the cardboard. Notice where all the dots are.
- Unbend a paper clip and use one of its ends to make an indentation on each of the dots. Be careful not to go all the way through the paper. You want to create bumps on the front side of the paper.
- Check your library for a book or other material written in Braille.
- Set out the Braille alphabet worksheet, Braille book, construction paper, pencil, and glue.

Introducing the Project

Show your children the Braille alphabet worksheet. Explain that people who are blind or who cannot see well can use this alphabet to read by feeling the raised dots. Each alphabet letter has a different set of dots to feel and read. Ask them if they have seen Braille letters anyplace else. Many public buildings and elevators have directions written in Braille.

The Project

Explain the following steps to your children.

1. Explore the Braille book with your fingertips.
2. Look at the Braille alphabet worksheet. Find and feel the letters in your name.
3. Select a sheet of construction paper.
4. Use a pencil to write your name in regular alphabet letters.
5. Trace over the letters with glue.
6. Set your paper in the designated place to allow the glue to dry.

Follow-Up

Pass out their name papers to the children. Ask them to close their eyes and slowly move their fingers across the letters in their names. Can they tell one letter from another with their eyes closed?

A	B	C	D	E	F
G	H	I	J	K	L
M	N	O	P	Q	R
S	T	U	V	W	X
Y	Z				

Let's Label That

Objective

Look for labels and the words on them.

Materials Needed

☐ worksheets
☐ index cards
☐ felt tip marker
☐ tape
☐ clipboard
☐ pencil

Setting Up the Station

• Make a copy of the worksheets on pages 69, 70, and 71 for each child.
• Use index cards and a felt tip marker to make labels that go along with the picture lists on the worksheet pages.
• Tape the labels to the appropriate items in your classroom.
• Set out a clipboard, a pencil, and copies of the worksheets.

The Project

Explain the following steps to your children.

1. Notice the labels all around the room.
2. Select one of the worksheets, attach it to the clipboard, and write your name on it.
3. Look at the first picture on the worksheet. Find the label on the matching item in the room.
4. In the space beside the picture on the worksheet, write the word from the label.
5. Repeat for the other pictures on your worksheet.
6. Continue with additional worksheets as time allows.

Follow-Up

Help the children make their own labels for items in the classroom.

Name_____

Name_____

Name

Word Collage

Objective

Learn that words are everywhere.

Materials Needed

❑ worksheet
❑ old magazines
❑ pencil
❑ scissors
❑ glue

Setting Up the Worksheet

• Make a copy of the worksheet on page 73 for each child.
• Collect some old magazines. Tear out pages that have words printed on them in large type.
• Set out the magazine pages, a pencil, scissors, glue, and copies of the worksheet.

The Project

Explain the following steps to your children.

1. Select a worksheet and write your name on it.
2. Look through the magazine pages and notice all the words on them.
3. Cut out the words you think look the best.
4. Glue the words to the worksheet to make a Word Collage.

Follow-Up

Help the children read the words on their collages. Ask them to notice things about their words. Can they find a short word? A long word? A colorful word? Do they have a tiny word on their collage? A giant word? Which word do they like the most? Hang up their Word Collages on a wall or a bulletin board.

My Favorite Words

Name_____

Read a Book

Objective

To learn about the written word in books.

Materials Needed

❏ worksheet
❏ construction paper
❏ scissors
❏ dictionary from pages 58-61
❏ stapler
❏ crayons
❏ pencil

Setting Up the Station

- Make at least one copy of the worksheet on page 75 for each child.
- Cut sheets of construction paper into fourths. Cut enough pieces so that there are two for each child.
- Find the dictionary you made for the Keyboards station on pages 58-61, or make it now. See directions on page 58.
- Set out the prepared dictionary, construction paper, stapler, crayons, a pencil, and copies of the worksheet.

Introducing the Project

Read a picture book to your children. Point out the words on each page. Talk about the way the words make up the story.

The Project

Explain the following steps to your children.

1. Select a copy of the worksheet.

2. Cut the squares out of the worksheet to make book pages.

3. On the bottom of each page, look at the unfinished sentence, "I like my__."

4. Look through the dictionary to find the picture and word for something you like.

5. Write that word on one of the pages. Draw a picture to go with it.

6. Complete the other three pages.

7. Arrange the pages in the order you like and add a construction paper cover.

8. Staple the pages together and write your name on the front.

Follow-Up

Set aside a time when the children can read their books to one another. Have them take home their books to read to their families. If you wish, copy extra worksheet pages for the children to take home to make additional pages for their books.

I like my _____.

I like my _____.

I like my _____.

I like my _____.

Recipes

Objective

"Read" and follow a written recipe.

Materials Needed

❑ recipe worksheet
❑ clear self-stick paper
❑ supplies for recipe

Setting Up the Station

• Select one of the recipe worksheets on pages 77, 78, and 79 and make a copy of it.

• Cover the copy of the recipe with clear self-stick paper (or have it laminated).

• Set out supplies for the recipe and the copy of the recipe worksheet.

Introducing the Project

Discuss recipes with your children. What are they? What do they do? Do the children's parents follow recipes when they cook? Talk about following directions. Explain that when they follow a recipe, they need to do each direction in order or the recipe will not turn out right.

The Project

Explain the following steps to your children.

1. Look at the recipe worksheet.

2. Wash your hands with soap and water, as it says in the first step.

3. Follow the remaining steps on the recipe to make your snack.

Follow-Up

Do the remaining two recipes during other station times. Make copies of the recipe worksheets to send home with the children. Make a class recipe book using the children's own unique recipes.

Funny Face Cracker

1. Wash hands.

2. Put graham cracker square on napkin.

3. Spread on peanut butter.

4. Add raisin eyes and nose.

5. Add an apple slice mouth.

6. Eat and enjoy.

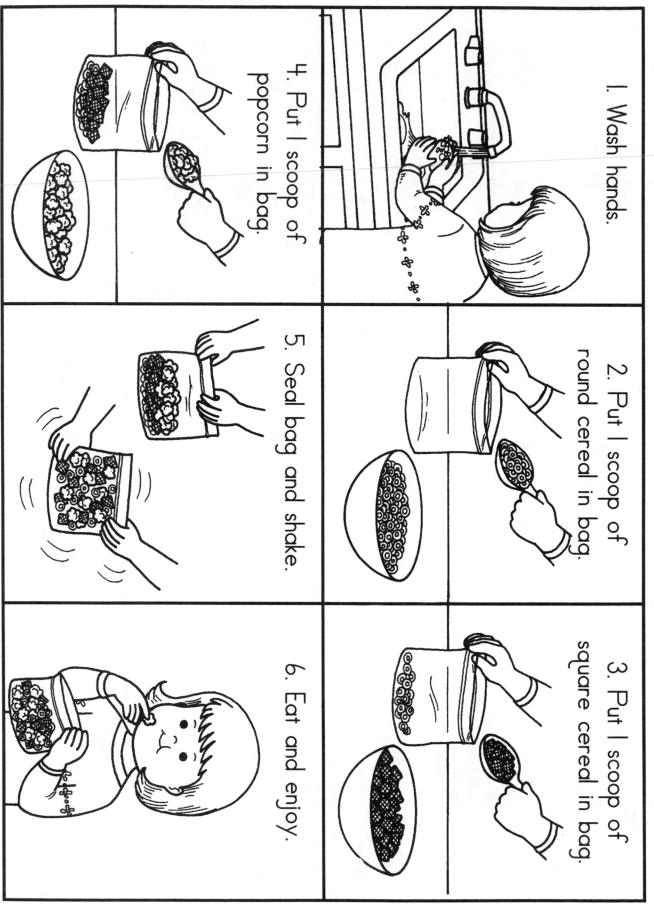

Trail Mix

1. Wash hands.

2. Put 1 scoop of round cereal in bag.

3. Put 1 scoop of square cereal in bag.

4. Put 1 scoop of popcorn in bag.

5. Seal bag and shake.

6. Eat and enjoy.

Fruit Salad

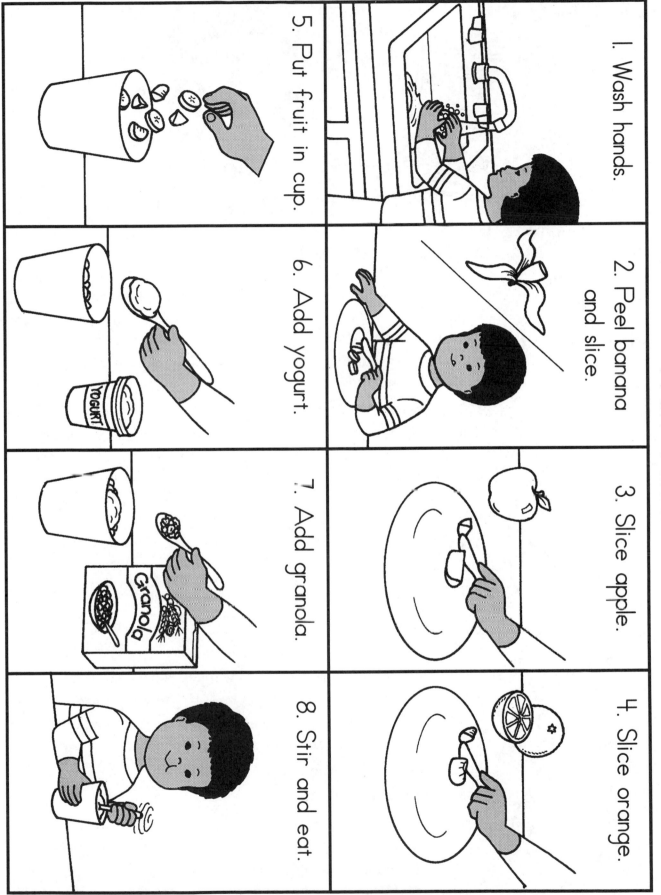

1. Wash hands.

2. Peel banana and slice.

3. Slice apple.

4. Slice orange.

5. Put fruit in cup.

6. Add yogurt.

7. Add granola.

8. Stir and eat.

Surveys

Objective

Take a survey and check the results.

Materials Needed

- ❏ worksheets
- ❏ clipboard
- ❏ pencil

Setting Up the Station

- Select one of the survey worksheets on pages 81, 82, or 83. Make a copy of the worksheet for each child, plus one for yourself.
- Fill out your copy of the survey worksheet for the children to look at as an example.
- Set out the completed survey example, clipboard, a pencil, and copies of the survey worksheet.

Introducing the Project

Tell your children that they will be taking surveys of what the other children in their class like. Then do a color survey with the children. Have them raise their hands when they hear you name their favorite color. Count the hands raised for each color, and write them down. Tell the children that they just helped you do a color survey. Which color was the most popular?

The Project

Explain the following steps to your children.

1. Look at the completed survey to see how it is done.

2. Take one of the survey worksheets and write your name at the top.

3. Clip the survey worksheet to the clipboard.

4. To fill out the first line, ask someone to tell you which of the four things on your survey is his or her favorite. Put an *X* below that item.

5. For the second line, ask a different person the same question. Put an *X* below that item on the second line.

6. Repeat with the remaining lines.

7. Put your survey in the designated place.

Follow-Up

Hand back the children's surveys. Look at their surveys together. Did everyone get the same answers? Help them compile all of their results. Which item was the most favorite? Which one was the least favorite?

Surveys

Name_____

Pet Survey	 🐕	 🐈	 🐦	 🐟
1				
2				
3				
4				
5				
6				

Permission to copy © 1998 Totline® Publications

Written Communication • Communication Station **81**

Name_____

Fruit Survey	🍎	🍌	🍇	🍉
1				
2				
3				
4				
5				
6				

Name_____

Recess Survey				
1				
2				
3				
4				
5				
6				

Can You Find This?

milk
eggs
peanut butter
bread

Objective
Practice using a list.

Materials Needed
❑ worksheet
❑ examples of lists
❑ pencil or crayon
❑ plain paper

Class List

Gina	Latisha
Katie	Rose
Troy	Garrett
Shaun	Trina
Ellie	Sidney
Ala	Michelle

Things to Do
- Feed Pets
- Put Toys Away
- Wash Hands
- Prepare Snack
- Sharpen Pencils

Setting Up the Station
• Make a copy of the worksheet on page 85 for each child.
• Collect a variety of lists, such as your class list, a grocery list, and a to-do list, and hang them up in the station.
• Set out a pencil or crayon, plain paper, and copies of the worksheet.

Introducing the Project
Ask your children what a list is. What does it do? It helps you remember things or it tells you what needs to be done. Have they ever used a list? Do they know anyone who has? What would they put on a grocery list if they were making one? Write their responses on a board. Let them think of other lists they might want to make.

The Project
Explain the following steps to your children.

1. Select a worksheet and write your name on it.

2. Look at the list of objects. All of the objects can be found in the picture.

3. Choose one of the objects and hunt for it in the picture.

4. When you find it, circle it in the picture and cross it off your list.

5. Choose another object to find. Continue until all of the objects have been found and crossed off your list.

6. If you wish, use the plain paper to make up a list of your own.

Follow-Up
Ask the children to tell you ways the list on the worksheet helped them find all of the pictures. (It helped them to know what items to look for, what items they had already found, how many items they had left to find, etc.) Help them make a list of the things they would like to do tomorrow.

Name_____

Find:

balloon block hat

boot kite apple

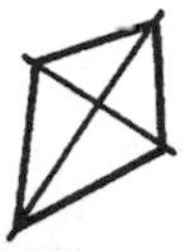

banana key pretzel

The Post Office

Your Communication Station becomes a post office with the activities
in this chapter. Let your children help you set out paper, envelopes,
pretend stamps, and other post office props. They could also help
make mailboxes and a post office counter. Then let the children enjoy
the hustle and bustle of a busy mailing center.

Here Comes the Mail

Objective

Understand how mail is sorted and delivered by the addresses on the envelopes.

Materials Needed

❑ cardboard milk cartons
❑ scissors
❑ tape
❑ worksheet
❑ permanent marker
❑ clear self-stick paper
❑ large shoulder bag
❑ envelope mailed to you

Setting Up the Station

- Decide how many mailboxes you would like to have. Collect that many half-gallon cardboard milk cartons.
- Turn each milk carton into a mailbox by cutting off the top and turning it on its side. Stack the cartons with the openings facing the same direction and tape them together.
- Make a copy of the worksheet on page 89 for each mailbox you have.
- Use a permanent marker to write a three-digit address inside one of the mailboxes, near the opening.
- Write the same address on the envelopes on one of the worksheet copies.
- Repeat for the remaining mailboxes and worksheet copiess.
- Cover the worksheet copies with clear self-stick paper (or laminate them). Cut out the envelopes.
- Put the envelopes in a large shoulder bag or "mail carrier sack."

Introducing the Project

Show your children an envelope that has been mailed to you. Point out your address on it. Tell them that the person who sent the envelope to you wrote your address on it so the mail carrier would know where to deliver the letter. Only envelopes with your address on them go into your mailbox.

The Project

Explain the following steps to your children.

1. Put on the mail carrier sack.
2. Take one of the envelopes out of the sack and read the number on it.
3. Put the envelope in the mailbox with the matching number.
4. Repeat with the remaining envelopes.
5. Collect all the mail you delivered and put it back in the sack for the next person.

Follow-Up

Ask the children to bring in envelopes with their address on them. Have them notice that all of the addresses are different. Help them read their address.

Wish You Were Here

Objective

Communicate through the mail.

Materials Needed

- ❑ worksheet
- ❑ large index cards
- ❑ black marker
- ❑ crayons
- ❑ pencil
- ❑ picture postcards
- ❑ postcard sent to you
- ❑ stamps

Setting Up the Station

- Make a copy of the worksheet on page 91 for each child.
- Give each child a copy of the worksheet to take home, requesting the address of a person to whom they would like to send a postcard. Set the completed forms aside.
- Find or purchase 4-by-6-inch unlined index cards. Turn the index cards into postcards by using a black marker to draw a vertical line on one side of the card to make the message side (left) and the address side (right).
- Complete one postcard by drawing a picture on the blank side. Turn the postcard over and write a message on the left side and an address on the right.
- Set out the prepared postcards, the completed postcard, crayons, and a pencil.

Introducing the Project

Show your children picture postcards you have collected. Talk about how post-cards are used to send quick notes to people. Ask if anyone has ever received a postcard. Who sent it? Did it come from a special place? Encourage them to think of things they might like to write on a postcard. Show them a postcard you have received. Point out the picture on the front and where the message and address are on the back.

The Project

Explain the following steps to your children. You may want to have an adult helper at this station.

1. Decide what message you would like to send.
2. On the plain side of the postcard, draw a picture.
3. On the other side of the postcard, on the left-hand side, sign your name near the bottom. If you want, write a short note above your name.
4. On the right-hand side, have an adult write the address of the person you are sending the postcard to, and help you put on a postage stamp. (Hint: If a child does not bring back an address, send it to his or her home address.)

Follow-Up

Take the children to a mailbox where they can mail their postcards. Have them bring in postcards they have received, and make a postcard mural.

Dear Parents,

    We will be designing, writing, and sending postcards to special friends and family. We need your help! Please write on the lines below the address of a person to whom your child would like to write.

    Thank you.

_____

Child's Name _____

Recipient's Name _____

Address _____

_____

_____

Greetings!

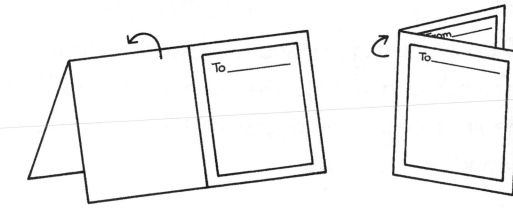

Objective

Send a message through greeting cards.

Materials Needed

- ❏ worksheet
- ❏ greeting card samples
- ❏ pencil
- ❏ crayons
- ❏ stickers
- ❏ rubber stamps
- ❏ ink pads

Setting Up the Station

- Make at least one copy of the worksheet on page 93 for each child. If possible, copy the worksheet onto several colors of paper.
- Hang up samples of greeting cards.
- Set out a pencil, crayons, stickers, rubber stamps, ink pads, and copies of the worksheet.

Introducing the Project

Show your children some of the greeting cards. Talk about the different times when a person might get a card: for a birthday, to feel better, to celebrate a holiday, to say "I love you," and so on. Have them think about the kind of card they might like to send to someone.

The Project

Explain the following steps to your children.

1. Look at the cards and see if you can tell what kind of occasion each one is for.
2. Decide what kind of card you want to send.
3. Select one of the worksheets and cut on the solid line to cut out the card.
4. Fold the card on the straight line first and then on the dotted line. (You might want to demonstrate this with one of the worksheets.)
5. Write the name of the person the card is for on the line that says "To."
6. Sign your name on the line that says "From."
7. Decorate your card with the materials provided.
8. Make additional cards, if you have time.

Follow-Up

Let the children show their cards. Have them tell what kind of cards they made and who they are for.

From

To

Design a Stamp

Objective

Create a new postage stamp.

Materials Needed

❑ worksheet
❑ envelopes with canceled postage stamps
❑ crayons
❑ pencil
❑ assortment of postage stamps

Setting Up the Station

• Make a copy of the worksheet on page 95 for each child.
• Collect envelopes with canceled postage stamps and hang them up in the station.
• Set out crayons, a pencil, and copies of the worksheet.

Introducing the Project

Show your children the assortment of postage stamps. The collection could include special series stamps available at the post office, stamps of different denominations, stamps from other countries, and stamps from years past. Have the children notice the variety of pictures and numbers written on the stamps.

The Project

Explain the following steps to your children.

1. Select a worksheet and write your name on it.
2. Look at the stamps on the envelopes.
3. Think about what you would want a postage stamp to look like.
4. Draw your design on the worksheet.

Follow-Up

Use the children's postage stamp designs to make a "Book of Stamps." Look at the book together.

Name_____

The Restaurant

Turn your Communication Station into a restaurant for the activities in this chapter. Let the children help you set out pretend food, plastic dishes and silverware, serving trays, aprons, chef's hats, and other restaurant props. Then add to your restaurant scene with the activities on the following pages.

Our Restaurant

Kindergarten Kitchen
Our Place
Mrs. Burn's Cafe
Our Restaurant

Objective

Communicate the name of the restaurant on a sign.

Materials Needed

❑ worksheet
❑ sheet of paper
❑ pen
❑ scissors
❑ crayons
❑ tape

Setting Up the Station

• Make a copy of the worksheet on page 99 for each child.

• Print the name of the children's restaurant (see Introducing the Project) on a sheet of paper and hang it up in the station.

• Set out scissors, crayons, tape, and copies of the worksheet.

Introducing the Project

Have your children think of names for their class restaurant. Write the names on a board or a large sheet of paper. Let them vote for their favorite name. This will be the name of their restaurant for the activities in this chapter.

The Project

Explain the following steps to your children.

1. Select a copy of the worksheet.

2. Cut out the sign shape.

3. Look at the example hanging up and print the name of the restaurant on your sign.

4. Decorate the sign.

5. Use the tape to hang your sign up somewhere in the station.

Follow-Up

Ask the children to name some restaurants they have seen or visited. Why do restaurants have names? What is the funniest restaurant name they have ever heard? What is the name of their favorite restaurant? Leave the signs up for other activities in this chapter.

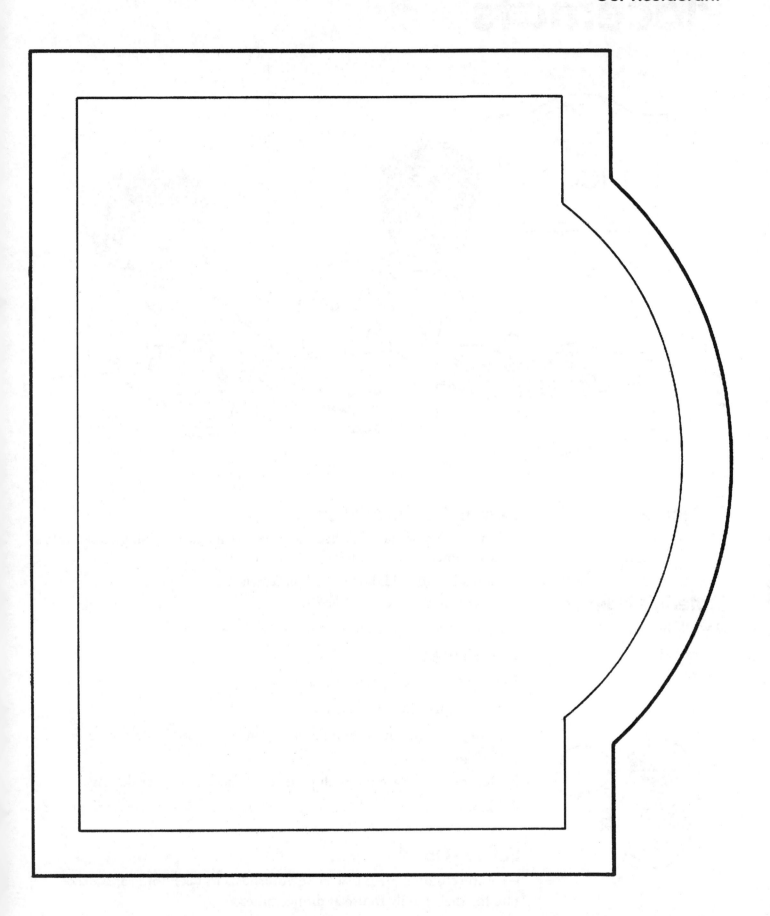

Placemats

Objective

Design placemats for the restaurant.

Materials Needed

❑ worksheet
❑ crayons
❑ box

Setting Up the Station

- Make a copy of the worksheet on page 101 for each child, plus extras to take home.
- Find a box to hold the finished placemats.
- Make sure there is a sign with the restaurant's name on it in the station.
- Set out the box, crayons, and copies of the worksheet.

The Project

Explain the following steps to your children.

1. Select a placemat worksheet.

2. Look at a sign with the restaurant name on it and write the name on your placemat.

3. Decorate the placemat with pictures of food and other designs.

4. Place your finished placemat in the box to use when setting the table at your restaurant.

Follow-Up

Give the children plain placemat worksheets to take home and decorate for their family to use at dinner time.

Here's a Menu

Objective

Make a menu and learn about communicating choices with it.

Materials Needed

❏ worksheet
❏ sample menus
❏ plain paper
❏ pen
❏ construction paper
❏ crayons
❏ scissors
❏ glue

Setting Up the Station

• Make a copy of the worksheet on page 103 for each child.

• Gather a variety of sample menus. Ask a local chain restaurant if they have a picture menu or a Braille menu you might borrow.

• Make sure there is a sign with the restaurant's name on it in the station.

• Set out the sample menus, construction paper, crayons, scissors, glue, and copies of the worksheet.

Introducing the Project

Show your children the sample menus. What is written on a menu? Why would a restaurant use a menu? What do the children like to order from a menu?

The Project

Explain the following steps to your children.

1. Look over the menus at the station.

2. Choose a sheet of construction paper and fold it in half to make a menu.

3. Look at a sign with the restaurant name on it and write the name on the front of your menu.

4. Select a copy of the worksheet and cut out the pictures and names of the foods you would like to serve at your restaurant.

5. Glue them to the inside of your menu.

6. Allow the glue to dry before using your menu in the restaurant.

Follow-Up

Divide the children into groups of two. Let them share their menus with their partners and practice ordering from them. Save the menus for the May I Take Your Order? activity on page 104.

hamburger

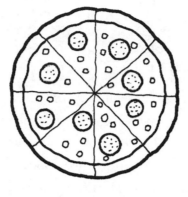

pizza

hot dog

sandwich

taco

french fries

spaghetti

salad

milk

soda pop

May I Take Your Order?

Objective

Communicate with a "customer" and write down the order.

Materials Needed

❑ worksheet

❑ scissors

❑ lightweight cardboard

❑ stapler

❑ pencil

❑ menus from pages 102-103

Setting Up the Station

• Make one copy of the worksheet on page 105.

• Write the name of the children's restaurant at the top of each food order form on the copy of the worksheet, and make ten copies of the worksheet.

• Cut the copies of the worksheet into individual food order forms.

• Cut lightweight cardboard into four 4½-by-5½-inch rectangles.

• Staple ten food order forms to the top of each cardboard rectangle to make a pad.

• Set out the order pads, a pencil, and completed menus from the Here's a Menu activity on pages 102-103.

Introducing the Project

Talk with your children about what happens when they are at a restaurant and they order something from the menu. What does their server do? Show them one of the order pads you prepared. Talk about how their food order is written down on an order form like this one. The form is given to the cook, who then knows exactly what food to prepare. The form also helps the server remember what food to bring back to each customer.

The Project

Explain the following steps to your children.

1. Working with a partner, decide who will be the customer and who will be the server.

2. The server hands the customer a menu.

3. The customer looks at the menu and decides what to order.

4. The server "writes" down the order as best as he or she can.

5. The server goes into the kitchen and brings out the imaginary food to the customer.

6. After the customer "eats," switch places and do it all over again.

Follow-Up

Talk about the roles the children played. Who liked being the customer best? Who liked being the server best? Keep the restaurant station stocked with food order pads for future role playing.

Book Project

Book Project

This yearlong activity is sure to become a treasured memory of your children's kindergarten experience. It starts on the first day of school and continues until the last.

As the children work on the pages for their individual books, they learn about communicating their thoughts and feelings through pictures and words. At the end of the year, they will each have 50 pages describing their kindergarten experience as seen through their own eyes.

Directions for Making the Book

1. Prepare a folder for each child so you can keep his or her pages together for future binding.

2. Of the following 50 pages, choose one whose topic goes with your lessons that day. Date the page and make a photocopy for each child.

3. Ask the children questions that will get them thinking about their responses and their drawings for the day.

4. Allow the children to have some quiet time to think about what they will draw.

5. Pass out the copies of the selected page to the children.

6. Let the children work on their pages.

7. As each child finishes, have him or her bring the page to you. If the drawing is not complete, encourage the child to work on it some more.

8. When the drawing is finished, have the child dictate his or her response to complete the sentence on the page. Write exactly what the child says.

9. Place each child's page in his or her folder.

At the End of the Year

1. Arrange each child's papers by date of completion, putting the title page "A Year in the Life of a Kindergartener" at the front.

2. Add a construction paper cover to each set of pages and staple them together to make a book. (Hint: Staple in a blank copy of the final page about the last day of school. Have the children finish this page after it is in the book.)

3. Let the children decorate the covers of their books.

4. Send the books home for everyone to enjoy.

A Year in the Life of
a Kindergartener

By _____

It's My First Day of School

On my first day of kindergarten, I feel _____

_____.

My Family

In my family, you will find _____

_____.

My Friends

My friends' names are _____

_____.

My School

I go to _____ School.

I Go to School

Today I came to school by _____

_____.

I Get Hungry

My favorite food is _____

_____.

I Get Thirsty

My favorite drink is _____

_____.

I Like to Read

My favorite book is _____

_____.

I Watch TV

My favorite TV show is _____

_____.

I Am Happy

I feel happy when _____

_____.

I Am Angry

I feel angry when _____

_____

I Am Sad

I feel sad when _____

_____.

I Am Excited

I feel excited when _____

_____.

I Am Surprised

I feel surprised when _____

_____.

I Am Frightened

I feel frightened when _____

_____.

I Am Bored

I feel bored when _____

_____ .

I Am Worried

I feel worried when _____

_____.

I Am Proud

I feel proud when _____

_____.

I Can Be Nice

I am nice when I _____

_____.

Sometimes I Forget the Rules

I forgot a rule when I _____

_____.

I Am Thankful

I am so thankful for _____

_____.

I'm Good at That

I am really good at _____

_____.

I Have Dreams

I had a dream that _____

_____ .

Make a Wish

I wish _____

_____ .

People Are Nice to Me

_____ was really nice to me when

_____.

When I Grow Up

When I grow up, I want to _____

_____.

I Love You

I love _____ very much.

You Love Me

_____ loves me very much.

It Is Fall

I know it is fall when _____

_____ .

It Is Winter

I know it is winter when _____

_____.

It Is Spring

I know it is spring when _____

_____.

It Is Almost Summer

I know it is almost summer when _____

_____.

My Kindergarten Teacher

_____ is my kindergarten teacher.

My Music Teacher

_____ is my music teacher.

My Physical Education Teacher

_____ is my physical education teacher.

My Art Teacher

_____ is my art teacher.

My School Librarian

_____ is my school librarian.

My School Counselor

_____ is my school counselor.

My Principal

_____ is my school principal.

_____

It Is Halloween

On Halloween, I dressed up like a _____

_____ .

Holiday Giving

I would like to give _____

a _____.

Holiday Gifts

My favorite present was _____

_____ .

Groundhog Day

On Groundhog Day, the groundhog _____

_____.

Valentine's Day

I like Valentine's Day because _____

_____.

Vacation Time

On vacation, I _____

_____.

My Birthday

On my birthday, _____

_____ .

The President

The President of the United States is _____

_____.

I Learned a Lot

In kindergarten, I learned _____

_____.

My Favorite Activity

My favorite thing to do in kindergarten was _____

_____ .

It's My Last Day of Kindergarten

Goodbye, kindergarten! On my last day, I feel _____

_____.

Totline® Publications

Teacher Books

BEST OF TOTLINE® SERIES
Totline Magazine's best ideas.
Best of Totline
Best of Totline Parent Flyers

BUSY BEES SERIES
Seasonal ideas for twos and threes.
Busy Bees—Fall
Busy Bees—Winter
Busy Bees—Spring
Busy Bees—Summer

CELEBRATIONS SERIES
Early learning through celebrations.
Small World Celebrations
Special Day Celebrations
Great Big Holiday Celebrations
Celebrating Likes and Differences

EXPLORING SERIES
Versatile, hands-on learning.
Exploring Sand
Exploring Water
Exploring Wood

FOUR SEASONS
Active learning through the year.
Four Seasons—Art
Four Seasons—Math
Four Seasons—Movement
Four Seasons—Science

GREAT BIG THEMES SERIES
Giant units designed around a theme.
Space • Zoo • Circus

KINDERSTATION SERIES
Learning centers for learning with language, art, and math.
Calculation Station
Communication Station
Creation Station

LEARNING & CARING ABOUT
Teach children about their world.
Our World • Our Town

MIX & MATCH PATTERNS
Simple patterns to save time!
Animal Patterns
Everyday Patterns
Holiday Patterns
Nature Patterns

1•2•3 SERIES
Open-ended learning.
1•2•3 Art
1•2•3 Blocks
1•2•3 Games
1•2•3 Colors
1•2•3 Puppets
1•2•3 Reading & Writing
1•2•3 Rhymes, Stories & Songs
1•2•3 Math
1•2•3 Science
1•2•3 Shapes

101 TIPS FOR DIRECTORS
Valuable tips for busy directors.
Staff and Parent Self-Esteem
Parent Communication
Health and Safety
Marketing Your Center
Resources for You
   and Your Center
Child Development Training

101 TIPS FOR PRESCHOOL TEACHERS
Creating Theme
   Environments
Encouraging Creativity
Developing Motor Skills
Developing Language Skills
Teaching Basic Concepts
Spicing Up Learning Centers

101 TIPS FOR TODDLER TEACHERS
Classroom Management
Discovery Play
Dramatic Play
Large Motor Play
Small Motor Play
Word Play

1001 SERIES
Super reference books.
1001 Teaching Props
1001 Teaching Tips
1001 Rhymes & Fingerplays

PIGGYBACK® SONG BOOKS
New lyrics sung to the tunes of childhood favorites!
Piggyback Songs
More Piggyback Songs
Piggyback Songs for Infants
   and Toddlers
Holiday Piggyback Songs
Animal Piggyback Songs
Piggyback Songs for School
Piggyback Songs to Sign
Spanish Piggyback Songs
More Piggyback Songs for School

PROBLEM SOLVING SAFARI
Teaching problem solving skills.
Problem Solving—Art
Problem Solving—Blocks
Problem Solving—Dramatic Play
Problem Solving—Manipulatives
Problem Solving—Outdoors
Problem Solving—Science

SNACKS SERIES
Nutrition combines with learning.
Super Snacks • Healthy Snacks
Teaching Snacks • Multicultural Snacks

THEME-A-SAURUS® SERIES
Classroom-tested, instant themes.
Theme-A-Saurus
Theme-A-Saurus II
Toddler Theme-A-Saurus
Alphabet Theme-A-Saurus
Nursery Rhyme Theme-A-Saurus
Storytime Theme-A-Saurus
Multisensory Theme-A-Saurus

TODDLER SERIES
Great for working with 18 mos–3 yrs.
Playtime Props for Toddlers
Toddler Art

Tot-Mobiles
Unique sets of die-cut mobiles for punching out and easy assembly.
Animals & Toys
Beginning Concepts
Four Seasons

Puzzles & Posters

PUZZLES
Kids Celebrate the Alphabet
Kids Celebrate Numbers
African Adventure
Underwater Adventure
Bear Hugs 4-in-1 Puzzle Set
Busy Bees 4-in-1 Puzzle Set

POSTERS
We Work and Play Together
Bear Hugs Health Posters
Busy Bees Area Posters
Reminder Posters

Story Time
Delightful stories with related activity ideas, snacks, and songs.

KIDS CELEBRATE SERIES
Kids Celebrate the Alphabet
Kids Celebrate Numbers

Parent Books

A YEAR OF FUN SERIES
Age-specific books for parenting.
Just for Babies
Just for Ones
Just for Twos
Just for Threes
Just for Fours
Just for Fives

BEGINNING FUN WITH ART
Introduce your child to art fun.
Craft Sticks • Crayons • Felt
Glue • Paint • Paper Shapes
Modeling Dough • Tissue Paper
Scissors • Rubber Stamps
Stickers • Yarn

BEGINNING FUN WITH SCIENCE
Spark your child's interest in science.
Bugs & Butterflies • Plants & Flowers
Magnets • Rainbows & Colors
Sand & Shells • Water & Bubbles

LEARN WITH PIGGYBACK® SONGS BOOKS AND TAPES
Captivating music with age-appropriate themes help children learn.
Songs & Games for Babies
Songs & Games for Toddlers
Songs & Games for Threes
Songs & Games for Fours
Sing a Song of Letters
Sing a Song of Animals
Sing a Song of Colors
Sing a Song of Holidays
Sing a Song of Me
Sing a Song of Nature
Sing a Song of Numbers

LEARN WITH STICKERS
Beginning workbook and first reader with 100-plus stickers.
Balloons • Birds • Bows • Bugs
Butterflies • Buttons • Eggs • Flags
Flowers • Hearts • Leaves • Mittens

LEARNING EVERYWHERE
Discover teaching opportunities everywhere you go.
Teaching House
Teaching Trips
Teaching Town

SEEDS FOR SUCCESS
Ideas to help children develop essential life skills for future success.
Growing Creative Kids
Growing Happy Kids
Growing Responsible Kids
Growing Thinking Kids

TIME TO LEARN
Ideas for hands-on learning.
Colors • Letters • Measuring
Numbers • Science • Shapes
Matching and Sorting • New Words
Cutting and Pasting
Drawing and Writing • Listening
Taking Care of Myself